Doodles Help Pre Handwriting

Sarah Muldoon, OTR/L

A Note About Pre Handwriting

From ages 3 to 5 years children begin to develop a lot of new cognitive functions. Three major area that show leaps in development are memory, noticing details, and sequencing. All three of these make this age a prime time for pre handwriting skill development.

Directed drawing is one of the best activities to foster these skills. These directed drawing exercises are special because they are made with pre handwriting in mind, using shapes or similar forms to what is needed for learning letter formation in kindergarten.

Coloring is also a very vaulable prewriting activity. It strengthens important intrinsic hand muscles, helps with visual perception and motor coordination, and fosters a love for visual arts.

My hope is that Doodles Help Pre Handwriting will develop the foundational skills that will translate to smooth sailing when learning handwriting and other important skills for school success, in kindergarten and beyond!

Happy tiny doodling!

For Rob and Katy

Mr. Sun

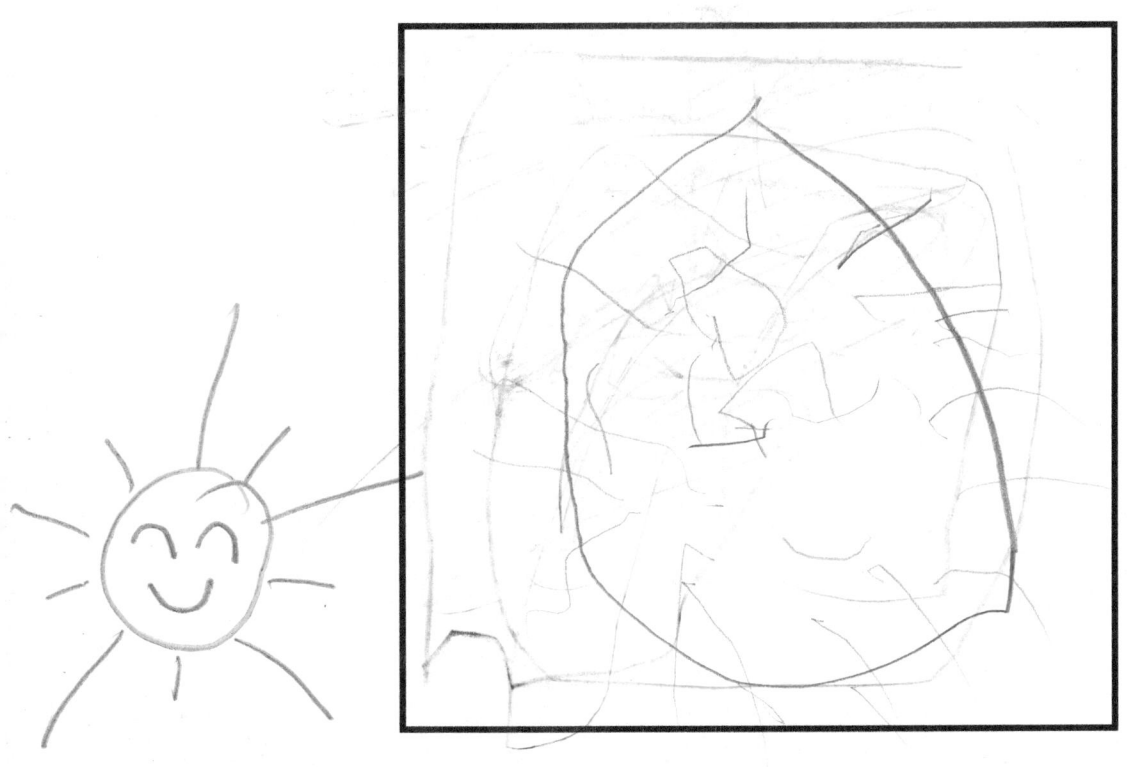

Flower

Avocado

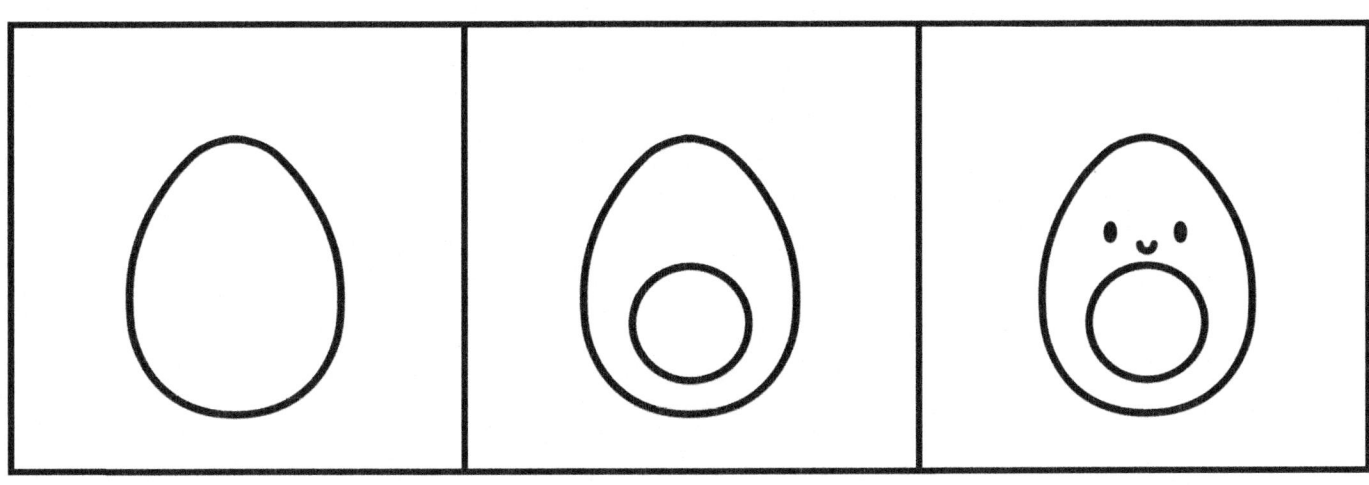

Baseball

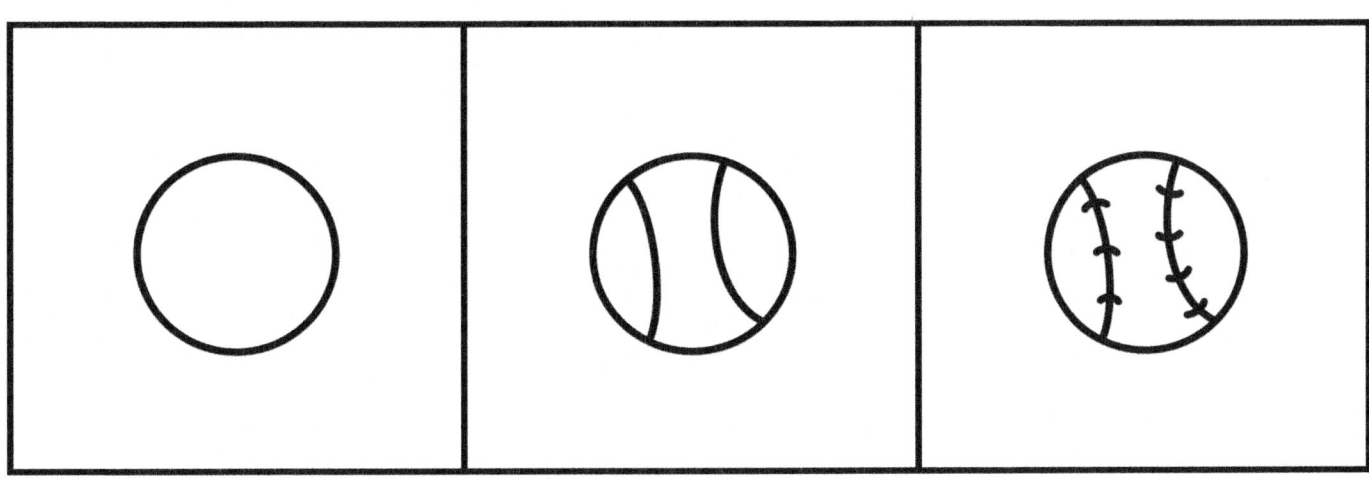

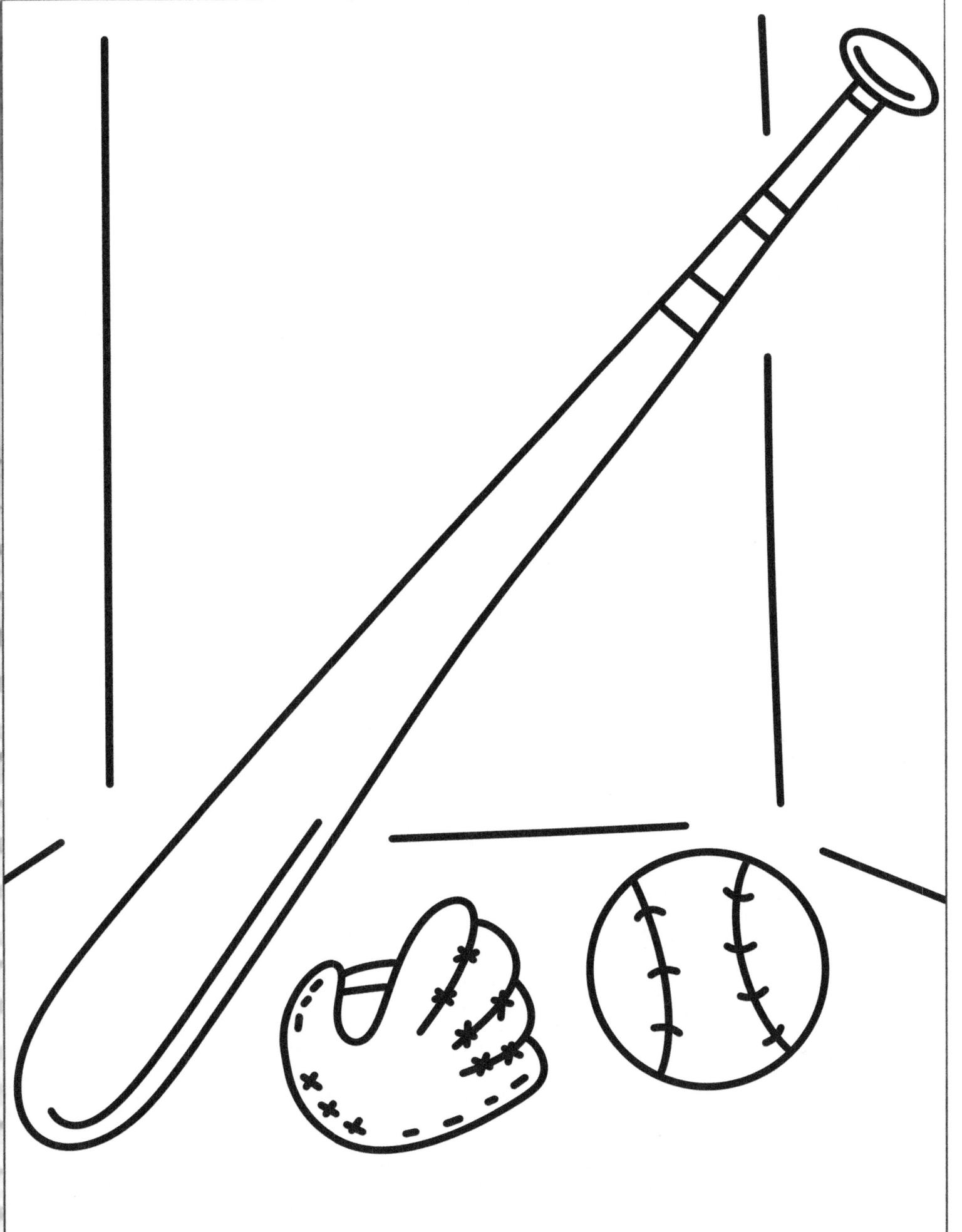

Candy

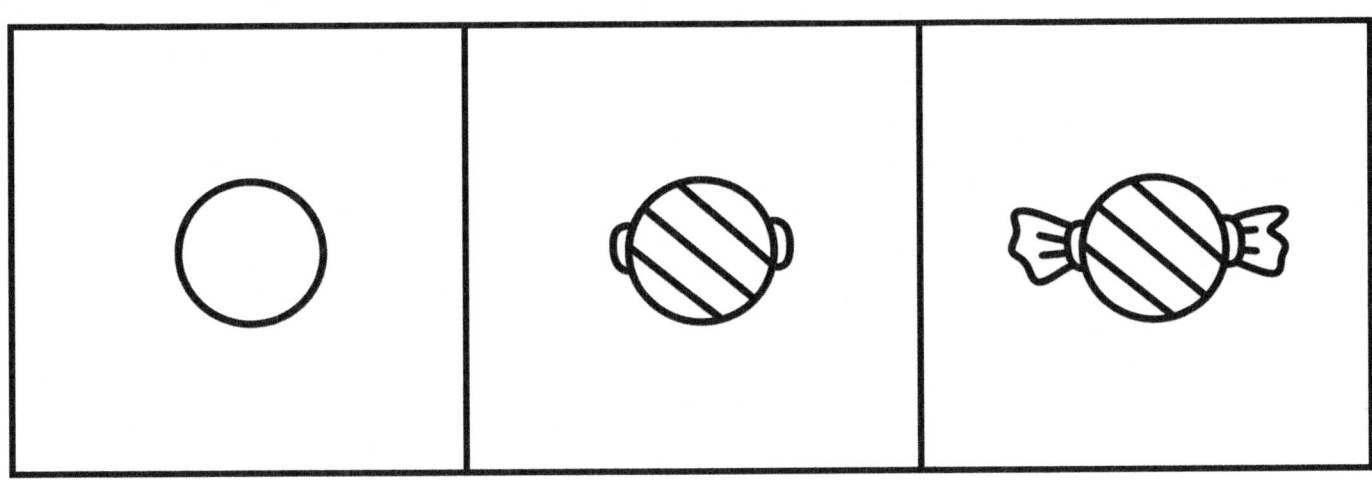

Chicken

Turtle

Mushroom

Bird

Jellyfish

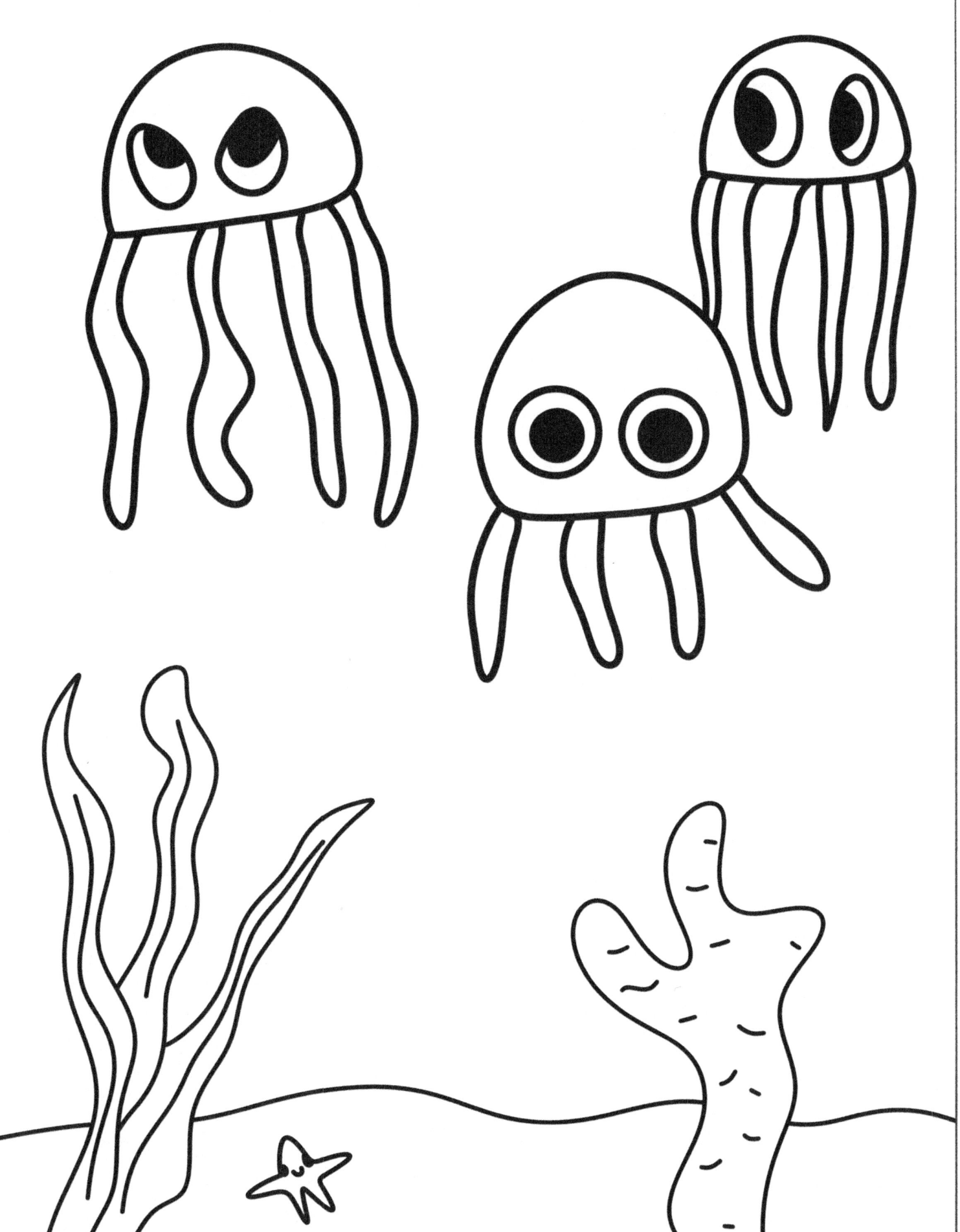

Popsicle

Cloud

Umbrella

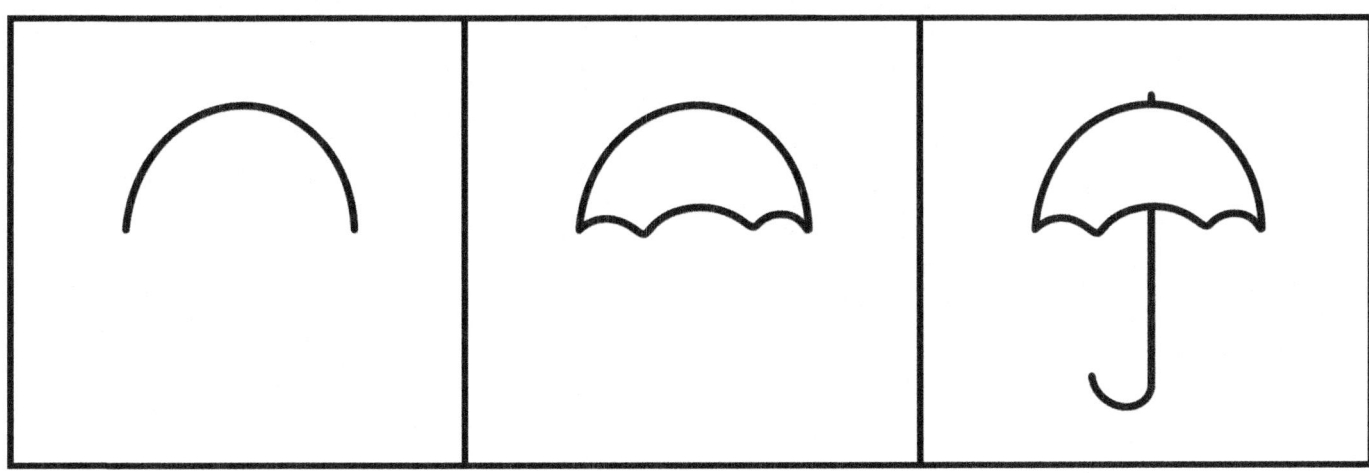

Cupcake

Bear

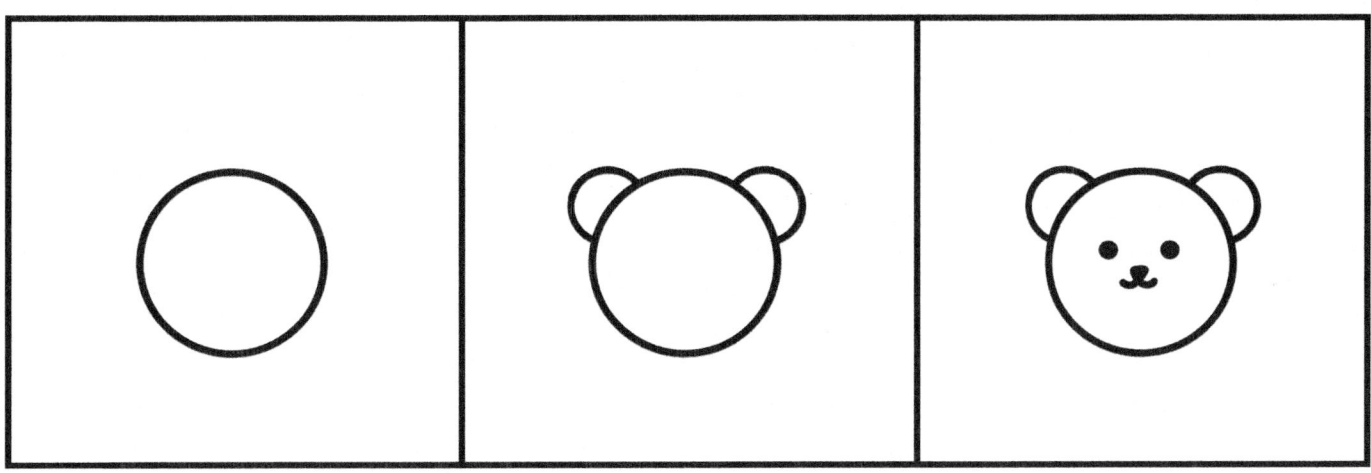

Sleepy Kitty

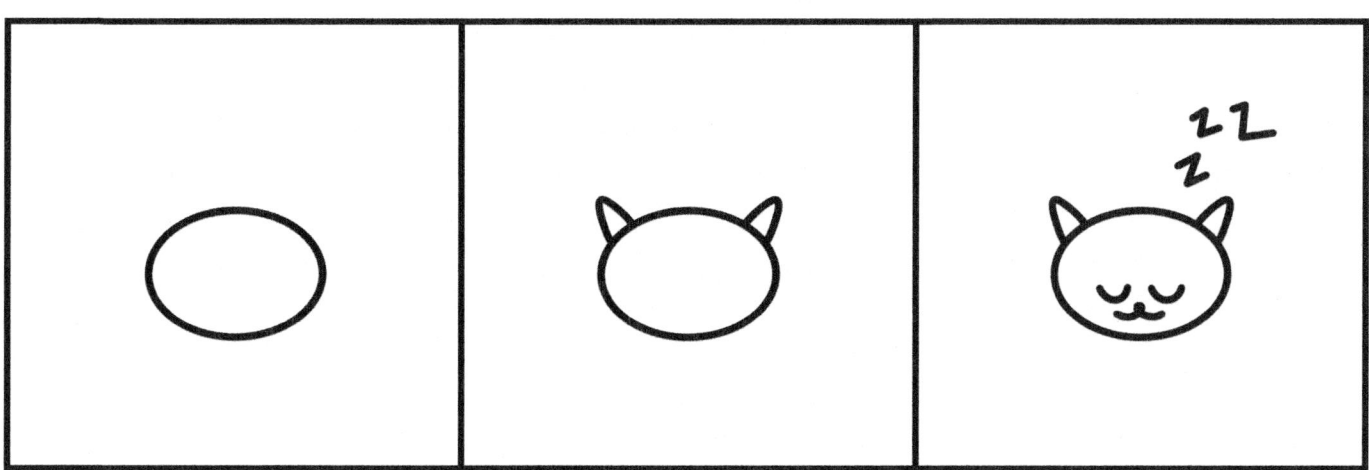

House

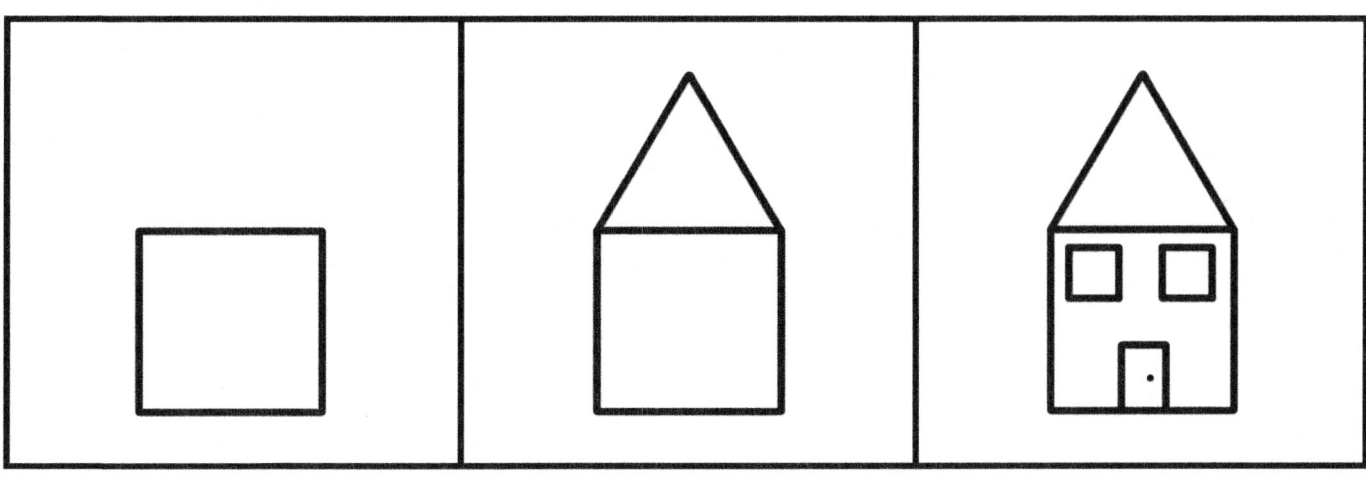

School

School Bus

Fish

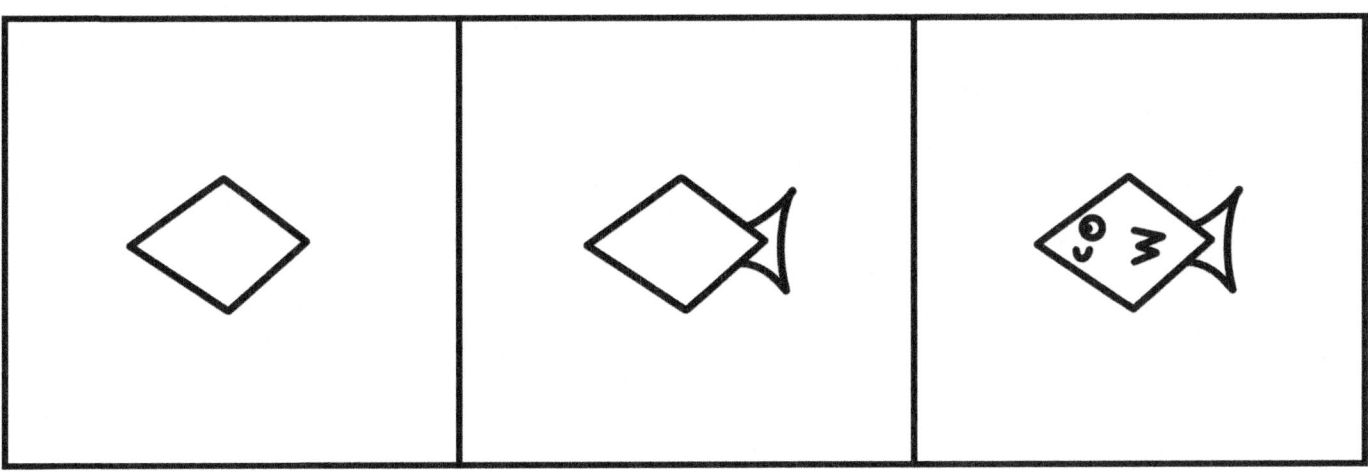

Pizza

Bulldozer

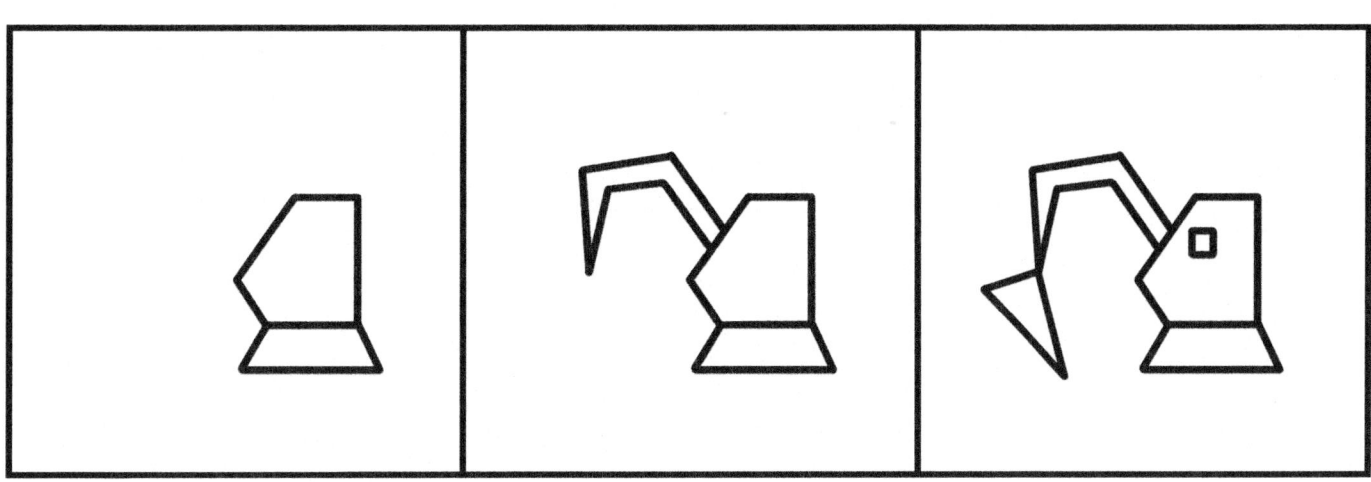

Present

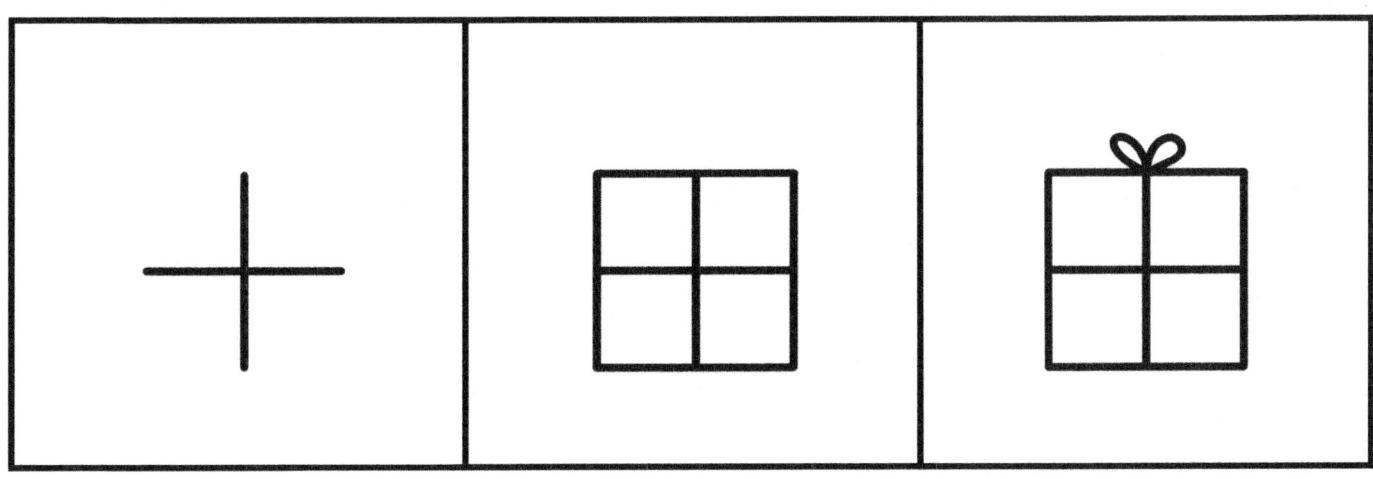

Kite

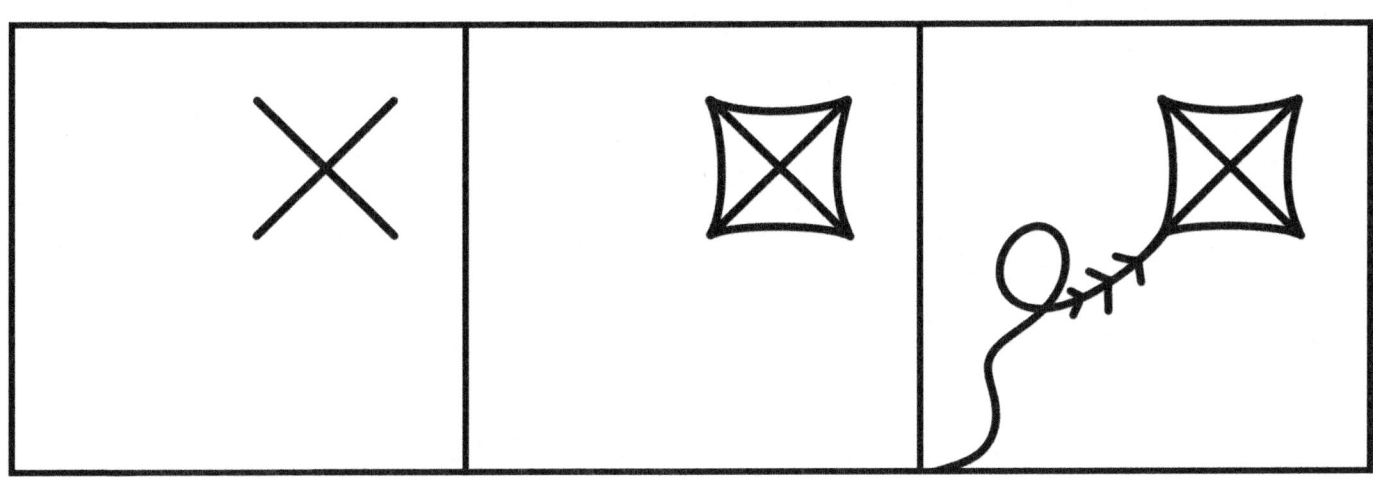

Make your own doodle

Make your own doodle

Make your own doodle

Make your own doodle

Make your own doodle

Printed in Great Britain
by Amazon